The
Interview Artist

Katrina Chretien

Copyright & Disclaimers

The Interview Artist by Katrina Chretien

c2016 by Katrina Chretien. All right reserved.

Gloucester & Midland Publishing

8107 Cooper Pass, San Antonio, TX 78255
or
GloucesterAndMidland@gmail.com

Cover Design: Dani Leoni
Editor & Publisher: Gloucester & Midland Publishing
Library of Congress Catalog Number: 2017932727
ISBN: 78-0-9985490-3-3
1. Career Development; 2. Self Help; 3. Resume Writing; 4. Interviewing
First Edition
Printed in the USA by CreateSpace, an Amazon.com Company

Dedication

This book is dedicated to my husband, Lawrence "Greg" Chretien, Jr. God blessed me by sending you into my life. When we united, he let you see deep into the hidden shadows of my soul. He gave you the spiritual guidance needed to orchestrate a beautiful, spiritual relationship with me. It was then that I could feel God's arms wrapped around us. I know that as long as you grant God the power to lead you, I can always feel secure in you leading me and our household.

For our spiritual obedience, God blessed us to become parents to not only, Joseph, but also to our miracle babies, both Kameron and Kennedy. That said, this work is also dedicated to our children. The four of you are forever special to me and I thank God for you.

Acknowledgments

This book is inspired by a score of men and women who have allowed me to assist in their career development. I hope that you continue to use the tools provided, to include saying a prayer before you embark on any new task. Always remember that once your career coach is always your career coach.

Not many people are as grateful as I am, to have not only been raised in a wonderful family and to have also married into one equally as awesome. I want to extend a special thanks to my parents, Nolan and Sylvia Vicks, for providing the initial platform to write and use my special gift from God. You encouraged me to put my feeling and thoughts on paper, whether it was in poetry, an essay, or a short story. Whenever the words won't flow orally, writing allows me an additional method to give God all the glory for both my trials and my triumphs. Thank you, God for my continuous cycle of miracles and blessings!

I also want to express my appreciation to my 8 siblings, my in-laws, extended family, and friends for the many moments of inspiration and encouragement for all my endeavors.

Lastly, I am forever grateful to all the instrumental people who were part of making this book a reality for me. You listened and heard my vision for this work, and invested your heartfelt talents in support of my goal. Your contributions are greatly appreciated.

Table of Contents

Foreword	6
Introduction	8
Chapter 1: Where Do I Start?	10
Chapter 2: The Faceless Introduction	13
Chapter 3: Put Your Face in Their Face	21
Cold Walks & Cold Calls	23
Email Blasts	25
Groups & Associations	28
Career Fairs & Career Services	29
Chapter 4: Finally Getting That Call- The Interview	35
Phone Etiquette	36
Voicemail Etiquette	40
Chapter 5: The Face to Face Meeting	43
The Preparation	44
Professional & Personal References	47
The Big Day	53
Cleanliness Is Next to Godliness	55
To Be Early….	55
The Wait is Over	57
Chapter 6: The Interview	59
Tool #1: Tell Me About Yourself	61
Tool #2: Concrete vs. Abstract	63
Tool #3: Targeted Selection	71
Tool #4: Questions & Answers	79
Chapter 7: I Got the Job, Now What?	83
Chapter 8: I Didn't Get the Job, Now What?	90
About the Author & Dear Reader	92-96

Foreword

"Katrina Chretien is an extraordinary individual with a passion for education specifically in Coaching and Career Development. She and I have had the pleasure of working together for 5 years in the past, where she was instrumental in encouraging others to see their full potential. We shared a common interest in developing minds with instrumental tools that will further their dreams and aspirations. Mrs. Chretien has always been adamant about career development and giving back to impact change and confidence in one's abilities and sharing her expertise in the field.

She brings a wealth of knowledge and expertise in the space that is informative and passionate. If you spend 5 minutes with her, you will quickly recognize the attributes and skills she brings to the table. I know her classroom research and her in-depth sharing of information at various college campuses as a career coach or mentor have further developed the skills of those she encountered. I have personally seen it firsthand was amazed at the tenacity and spirit de corps she has.

Her skills and her level on intense knowledge and understanding in career coaching and development is a valued asset to any person or organization. Katrina is an excellent communicator both orally and in writing context. He demonstrates an outstanding ability to interpret literature by bringing the content in to undefined space and shares an intellectual and understanding aspect to those that encounter her.

In terms of sheer spirit and intellect to deliver powerful and impactful presentations, she can set a room on fire with her contagious smile and personality. When given the opportunity, she can creatively challenge people to think beyond status quo and indulge in poignant conversation that challenges how they think. She understands how to reach within and open their minds and thoughts to meet the challenge of the next level.

Katrina has and always will serve as a servant leader. It is who she is and always will be. She understands that greatest gift we can give to others is to give freely of that which can impact them socially, economically, and academically, without expectation of anything in return. She makes those she is serving, the most important people in the room.

With a superlative mind, she will complete her task. Katrina commands attention by virtue and brilliance of her integrity to give her all. She is well-versed and extremely knowledgeable of career development and coaching. Her acquired knowledge in the many classroom hours and multiple years of working in the field in various positions, gives her insight and understanding in that which is current and relevant.

My encounters with Katrina Chretien, as we worked together, allowed us to build a bond and friendship that I will forever cherish. If you're ever looking for an understanding Career Development Coach for a classroom or an organization, this book is highly recommended. Any works of Katrina Chretien is your best choice."

John C. Williams, Jr., EMBA
Chief Business Development Officer
Ronco Energy, Dallas, TX

Introduction:

The workplace is filled with haves and have nots. What I mean is that there is a plethora of men and women just like you and me that have either secured employment of some sort, or they have not. They make up our entire population and those who have secured employment fill positions of every possible occupation known to man-from an apprentice to a zoo keeper and all those in between.

While qualifications play a huge part in job security, we often look at others and wonder a series of thoughts as to how that person got their job; especially when we deem ourselves as the best fit.

When that happens, have you ever found   yourself contemplating these questions?

-How did they really get that job?
-Did they know someone (or got a family hook up)?
-Are they bribing or blackmailing someone?

Don't be ashamed. It is natural to find reasons to discredit someone when they may have been the person hired or promoted instead of you.

This thought process is our own personal and initial self-soothing mechanism, before we accept the truth. The truth hurts, but it's time to face it. You were neither qualified nor the best fit.

In the following chapters, I will show you that you don't have to know someone (although networking is very beneficial) or compromise your integrity to secure employment in the field of your choice and within scope of your qualifications.

Chapter One:

Where Do I Start?

CH1: Where Do I Start?

Sure, it is easy to say start at the beginning, but where is that exactly? You should start here.

 -**Determine if this is a job or a career search.** Yes, there is a difference. A job search indicates that you are seeking temporary work. You know, the I just need something to tie me over to pay the bills type of work. A career search dictates that you are seeking a long-term commitment. This is typically a field of passion. Usually you have gone to school or invested in on-the-job training to establish this type of work. A career job feels effortless and you enjoy it. It is the work from which you plan to retire or drop dead doing it because you are so heavily invested with passion. It is imperative that you understand that whether you are a job seeker or a career seeker, all my principles can be applied to your launch.

  -**Be qualified**. Let's be realistic for a moment. If you have only a 12th grade education, is it prudent of you to apply for a brain surgeon position at your local medical center? Okay, so I over exaggerated a bit, but to my point, it is in your best interest to avoid setting yourself up for disappointment and failure. Take yourself and your employment goals seriously.

  -If you are not completely qualified, how can you gain experience if no one would hire you? This is such an agonizing part of the job and career search. Most college and career school graduates experience this often. Throughout the secondary education experience, your eye is on the prize/goal.

The plan is to graduate with a degree(s) or certification(s) and have a confirmed position with a great employer the next day. How many of us think beyond that? Not many. While advance education is never a bad decision, students travel through their curriculum being repeatedly fed most of the fluff and pros of the industry or the position with focus primarily on the income.

Very often, those professors and instructors who are providing this positive re-enforcement to students have somehow forgotten where they came from. How can they forget starting at the bottom and gradually building their careers? They have forgotten to tell students that although the engineering field, for example, is financially lucrative, they may have to accept the first job offer at $35k to start gaining experience and building their resumes instead of the $125k they kept referring to the entire program.

They have forgotten to tell that having a college degree or certification will not guarantee immediate hire, so I will tell you. Brace yourself to make some initial sacrifices for your career launch.

Chapter Two:
The
Faceless Introduction

CH2: The Faceless Introduction

This chapter will explain many of the resume DO NOTS. To make my point, I must share a story that I like to call, "Don't Be A Bud."

Many years ago, I worked as the human resources manager for a government contract in Dallas, Texas. While there, I gained many friends that have remained friends since the contract ended. One of those friends was a member of our management team, who I will call Bud. When I met Bud, he was 63 years old. He had retired twice in his career-once from the military and again from a prestigious aerospace defense company.

After the government contract ended, Bud found himself in a bit of a situation. Society was trying to dictate his retirement. He was not yet ready to retire, so he pursued other employment without success and a few consulting opportunities of interest. After several months of networking and submitting his resume around the area, he grew frustrated. He then reached out to me for help. He explained to me that he didn't understand why a man of his credentials was having such a hard time finding new work. He requested that I take a look at his resume and give him some feedback and pointers where needed.

A few days after our conversation, he emailed me his resume. Due to my hectic schedule, I didn't get a chance to review his document right away, so it sat in my inbox for nearly 2 weeks. After a very long day at work and having worked late (until 11pm), I managed to get home and just wanted to crash. I didn't care that I had not eaten all day. I just wanted to sleep, but a little voice told me to check my email, which I did. Awaiting me was a follow up email from Bud.

Because he had been waiting so patiently for nearly 2 weeks, I felt bad and said to myself, "I need to just get this done for him." In that late moment, I decided that I was going to bite the bullet and take care of the resume issue for Bud, so I double clicked the attachment to open the document. It did not open immediately. My curser just kept circling. As my laptop was timing and trying to download Bud's resume, I got tired of waiting and used the wait time to take a shower and even a quick bite to eat.

After completing my bedtime routine, I returned to my laptop to delve into my project, but I couldn't. My computer was still timing and downloading. I grew frustrated and just as I was about to close the program, it opened. Boy, did it open and with great surprise!

As I sat in front of the computer screen, there was a picture of Bud staring back at me. He was about 27 years old and wearing his military uniform. Let me be clear of the emphasis here. How old was Bud when I first met him? Yes, he was 63 then and 6-7 years later at or near age 70, he was using a picture of himself during his twenties. Bud had not looked like the man in the photo since he took the photo. Now, imagine him circulating his resume with that picture.

Let's not think about the rest of the resume for a minute. Based on picture alone, when Bud would receive calls for an interview and showed up to said meeting, what do you think was happening? The man walking through the door was not the man on paper. Bud's resume also included a biography below his snapshot which stated his full name, contact information, race (although his picture was obvious), sexual orientation, religious affiliation, spouse's name, how many children and grandchildren he had, to also include that some of his children were adopted.

I figured the photo was the sole cause for such a long download, but it was not. Bud had sent me a 15-page resume, which encompassed every single job he has ever had in his life. Once I realized that he sent me a magazine to review, I emailed him back and said, "Bud, I finally had a chance to view your resume, but I need time to really go through it because IT DOES NEED WORK. I need to figure out reducing size without losing pertinent information."

By the time I completely reviewed Bill's resume, which was about a week later, I was able to reduce his resume to 3 pages without pictures and his unprofessional biography, while still presenting the best of his skills summary.

Afterwards, I grew pensive and curious. I was trying to figure out how had he successfully secured employment with that resume for all those years. Finally, I arrived at this conclusion and logic.

Bud was from the old school. During his high school and college years, he was taught that everything he included on his resume was correct. Nothing was off limits. There were no boundaries between the employer and the applicant. The reason Bud had not had any problems securing employment in the previous 45-50 years was because the people who were hiring and interviewing him were also from the old school, so their resumes probably looked just like his. Of course, they wouldn't see a problem with his.

Now, let's fast forward to the 20th century where recruiters, human resources professional, and hiring managers are made up of people half Bud's age, which means they that they were taught that everything about Bud's resume is now considered as the "RESUME DO NOTS". Bud's curriculum vitae was a flood zone of present-day discrimination for age, race, religion, creed, sexual preference, and the list could continue.

That said, here is a short summary of ideas to keep in mind when constructing your resume:

Use traditional, standard paper in white or neutral colors. If you must use anything other than white, I suggest colors in off white, beige or tan, and gray. Anything else is too flamboyant and distracting.

Avoid scented paper for two reasons: 1. It serves no purpose unless you are writing a love letter to someone special, which in this case would be totally unprofessional. 2. Unaware of another person's allergies, you may be upsetting the manager or recruiter's day with constant sneezing and watery eyes as they paper screen applicants. This alone could prevent your resume from being selected for further consideration.

Use a traditional font and font size. We all have our preferences, but I recommend that you choose font size twelve (12) between either fonts, Times New Roman, Arial, Tahoma, or Calibri.

Don't try to outline your entire life in the document. It is neither your autobiography nor a magazine feature story. Your resume should capture the last 7-10 years of your work history. There are exceptions for times when you may be pursuing a career or industry change.

In that case, you may need to move something around to highlight your experience and skills in that arena if it surpasses the 7-10 year window.

Don't make the recruiter or manager search for your applicable skills. Recruiters receive multiple resumes and applications per day. To fill one position, they may receive 100 or more. Clearly, time won't be spent interviewing all 100 candidates, so the narrowing process starts.

Each resume will receive the initial 10-15 second paper screen, which includes a quick glance for highlighted skills that are associated with the position to be filled. Their goal is to identify the top 3- 10 people to pre-screen. These are the 3-10 resumes that get read in their entirety.

The pre-screen method, usually conducted by phone, an online screening test, or even with an in-person meeting, is a brief, 15-30 minute initial interview to further narrow the list of 3 to10 candidates to the best 3-5 whom will move forward to a face-to-face meeting. So, if you want to be among that lucky 3-5 interviewees, make sure your skills pop out from the page at the pre-screener. Do not list your skills summary at the bottom of your resume. They will never get viewed in the paper pre-screen phase.

Ensure that you are the person that you are describing on your resume. There is no reason to lie about who you are and your abilities because you will get busted.

Own who you are, market the best of yourself and what you have to offer to an employer. This is also the same for those who may have concerns with disclosure of background check convictions.

Please understand that a wise person can avoid mistakes by learning from someone else's mishaps. While Bud's story is hilarious to share, it is real. Resumes like his old-school adaptation are still floating out there in society and those people are still wondering why they aren't getting interviews.

As for my friend, Bud, he received more interview calls from his updated resume, but never got an actual job offer. He found that society was still trying to place him in a box of retirement against his will for the 3rd time.

He decided to venture out on his own and became a successful self-employed government consultant. To date, he is doing well and enjoying the freedom and flexibility of being an entrepreneur.

Chapter Three:

Put Your Face
In Their Face

Ch3: Put Your Face in Their Face

Today, the most traditional work search method is via internet. There are multitudes of popular job search sites on the worldwide web. There are great resources for your initial resume blast, but don't rely solely on the internet to secure your employment goal. It is so easy to get caught up in hiding behind the computer screen. This is not enough for a few reasons.

Recruiters spend a large amount of their time sourcing candidates and screening resumes. It could be what seems like forever before they get to yours and who's to say that they select you for that initial pre-screen interview.

Several human resources recruiters and staffing agencies advertise what is referred to as "blind postings". This is the little secret method they use to maintain a constant flow of candidate resumes in their pipeline for positions that are not open or available during that time. It is a great method for the organization, but a waste of time for you, the applicant.

For you, the annoyance with this is never knowing whether a posting is active or blind, so apply anyway, but don't stop there. I want to show you ways to put your face in their face. Pay attention to the multiple ways you can get your face into their face.

Cold Walks & Cold Calls

I am a huge fan of being one with the people. So, networking is something I enjoy, but not many share my sentiment. Sometimes, an employer doesn't know they need you until they meet you; therefore, you must put your best foot forward to start making your face and name known within the industry.

There are several ways to network and market yourself in the business world. I personally recommend cold walking and cold calling employers of interest. It only takes a moment to reach them (usually their human resources department) and inquire about current or forecasted opportunities. Most will refer you to their websites, but this is helpful if you have previously visited their site and found nothing available or of interest.

The human resources department is always aware of roles that may be opening later, whether it is due to either a pending termination, or company growth or restructure. This is the cold call process.

A cold walk is very similar, but instead of calling the employer, you get dressed as if you are scheduled for an interview, be prepared with a folder full of resumes, and you approach the front desk or

HR department with audacious confidence. Once there, you request to speak to a manager or an HR professional. Naturally, you will be asked if you have an appointment. You don't have to lie about having an appointment. Your response should sound something like the *example below.*

"Good Morning/Afternoon. My name is _____ and I was hoping to speak with a manager or HR professional about current job opportunities in the _____ department."

Now, don't be caught off guard when the front desk receptionist looks at you with wide eyes and uncertainty of how to proceed. Once he/she gathers their thoughts, they will either immediately tell you that you need an appointment to see a manager, need to go to their websites to view job openings (to include possibly that their HR department isn't located locally), or they just might call a manager to the front desk and allow you a chance to briefly speak with them. If the latter happens, you have to make it count for all it is worth. Don't forget that sometimes an employer doesn't know they need you until they meet you.

So, what do you do when the manager appears? What do you say? How do you act? First of all, you should smile and extend your hand to offer a firm; yet professional handshake. Introduce yourself and hand them a copy of your resume packet. In the interim, express that you are currently an active job/career seeker and interested in securing an opportunity with their company in the position of choice. Use this time to quickly express one highlight of your professional assets that qualify you to be considered. For example:

"Good Morning/Afternoon, my name is _____ and I am a recent graduate from ABC University with a bachelor degree in Marketing. I was fortunate to complete an unpaid internship for the past 3 summers at XYZ Resorts in their sales & marketing department, where I sold event and catering packages for corporate and civic events. Are you currently hiring for your sales & marketing department?"

You will know if you have piqued the manager's interest if they pursue further conversation by either inviting you to an impromptu meeting in their office or if they schedule you to return to discuss opportunities and your experience.

Email Blast

Back in the day, the telephone book was my ultimate resource for information. While the internet was available, many household didn't have access; not to mention, web time was billed to the telephone bill, so I had to watch my pennies and avoid luxury expenses. As I was launching my career, I basically stalked employers via phone and fax.

That was a tedious process, but it worked at that time. I would spend hours researching the phone books of my tri-parish areas and metropolitan cities for employers of interest. Imagine calling a list of 75-100 businesses and asking the same questions over and over.

"Hello, may I speak to a manager or someone in your human resources department?"

During those days, it was easier to either speak to a person of authority or to be given their contact information. Today, it is an act of congress to be provided information via phone; therefore, your research must intensify to find out who's who in the company hierarchy and how to contact them. If you don't make yourself a priority, you should not expect anyone else to do so. That said, I now put on my professional hat of ambition and get to searching the world-wide-web for whatever and whomever I want.

Let me simplify this. For my former students, graduates, and clients, I source employers in a specific industry, in a specific area. One by one, I visit their websites and find a list of their staff, crossing my fingers that their individual contact information is listed (i.e phone number and email address).

While my focus is for the resume to land in the hands of either a hiring manager or the human resources department, I audaciously send said resume to every single person in the organization that has an email address provided on the website. Some would say that I wasted a lot of time, but I view it as I invested a lot of time for something important to me or important to the person I am assisting.

Here is my logic. While everyone who receives my resume is not my person of interest, my hope is that they ultimately say to themselves,

"Hmmm. I am not hiring in my department, but let me forward this to so-and-so in the XYZ department who may be interested in this candidate."

I know this is a nuisance for them, but I appreciate the ones who respond to my email with further guidance for my cause like redirecting me to managers who are hiring or to the human resources department.

I was assisting a college graduate who was trying to relocate from Louisiana to Texas to launch her social work career. While she was preparing to go to graduate school, she still wanted to embark on her passion of human services, primarily working with children and young adults.

As her career coach, I was extremely proactive in acquiring a list of all human services and non-profit entities in the Houston area for her. Immediately I implemented my email blast process. I went so far as to send her resume to over 50 people in the same organization and 3 of them responded with request to set up an interview.

She was fortunate as she utilized all my interviewing techniques and was hired a week later. This result varies for each person, but I want to point out that doing your due diligence eventually pays off.

Groups & Associations

Word of mouth is the most popular form of recruiting. Employers have confidence that if one of their employees refer someone to work there, that employee is making 2 bold statements:

1. *They like and enjoy working there as they would not refer a friend to a place that they themselves hate; and*

2. *The employee is not going to risk their name and reputation in the company by referring someone that they really don't trust to be qualified and able to perform the job duties.*

If you are a member of any social, civic or professional organization or clubs, make your membership (and dues) benefit you to the fullest. During meetings, make a point to mention that you are in process of launching or re-booting your career and would appreciate if anyone could provide some leads for positions in your preferred industry. I have found that this is especially beneficial within greek and social organizations.

Don't fret if you are not in a fraternity or sorority as there are several organizations within each community that can serve the same purpose. Industry groups and unions are also a good place to network.

Many people don't think of the unemployment office as a viable resource, but you would be surprised. Dealing with the unemployment office or your local workforce commission is much easier than it was 20 years ago. We now live in a society where you can hide behind the computer screen to apply for unemployment benefits and peruse their active list of jobs in the community.

Networking through this venue doesn't have to be an embarrassment. Your tax dollars allow you to be loud and proud about utilizing resources that will assist you in your career growth.

Career Fairs & Career Services

Whether it is a community or college fair, you have a great opportunity at your fingertips. First, these events will host some on the key people you want to meet and talk to-Hiring Managers & HR Recruiters. Much like the blind posting technique, job fairs allow companies to maintain a candidate pipeline if they are not actively hiring.

If they are indeed hiring, this gives them a chance to pre-screen candidates, not only on paper, but also visually. They are provided an opportunity to briefly speak with candidates and schedule further meetings if interested. When attending a job or career fair, treat it as you would a cold walk and have fun networking.

If you have a difficult time finding local fairs to attend, you can always check the following resources to see if they are hosting any scheduled events:

-The Unemployment Office
- Community Centers
- Area Hotels & Event Centers
-Local Colleges & Universities

College and University Career Service departments typically host at least two career fairs per school year-one in the Fall Semester and the other in the Spring. Career Schools provide their students and graduates the same, but I am certain that they host at least one per year. When it comes to your Career Services department, USE THEM!! I cannot stress this enough. USE THEM!

Traditionally on a college or university campus, that department will not run behind you to utilize the resources they offer. It is up to you to be proactive and find out what they can offer. Not only do they organize the campus job fairs, but they also provide career coaching and job placement assistance. They also host area employers who may be interested in conducting on campus interviews for their available positions.

Career Schools are a little different in that the company, at large, relies heavily on the career services department to assist graduates with job placements.

The difference between career services at a career school and a traditional college is based solely on the career school's need to validate themselves to maintain accreditation.

To provide validity that their programs are valuable to the community and students, they must prove that 70% or more of their graduates are securing employment in their respective fields of study. If they are unable to do so, they risk losing the accreditation for the program(s), which can also lead to the school's demise and closure. I experienced this with a former employer. It broke my heart that my hard work and investments were invalid after 3 years of labor as the school lost its' credentials and ultimately closed its' doors. Now, it was not that black and white. There were some other bigger issues that led to the school's closure, but it has no relevance to my point.

Your career services representatives should be well versed in interview etiquette, resume writing, mock interviewing, job recruiting and placement. If you find that the person assisting you is a little laxed in your efforts to help you, it could mean one or two things, if not both.

They are either unqualified for their role or not happy in their role. If they are unqualified, that's one thing. They are simply the product of lack of knowledge and were lucky enough to get hired. These representatives can't provide you with what you need if they are clueless.

If they are qualified, but unhappy with their employer or their role, they won't be truly invested in you and your success because they are trying to get themselves out their situation. These are the people you have to beware of because instead of job searching for you, they will be
looking for themselves and could possibly snatch a few job leads that were intended for you.

During my junior year in college, I still had no idea that career services existed. I accidentally learned of them. One day as I was leaving school, I took a short cut through the student union to the parking lot. At that time, there was construction going on at the campus, so many offices were getting shifted around temporarily. Through the student center to the parking lot, I had to also walk through the ballroom.

Well, wouldn't you know it. I notice a door that read, "Career Services," so I entered to be nosey. Two mature ladies stood up from their desks in shock that I entered. One asked, "How can we help you, Hun?" In my state of awesome wonder, I stood there gazing at the various job boards, tables filled with career magazines and pamphlets, and the federal employment law posters. It was ironic because I was hoping to leave one of my three mall jobs during that time.

Finally, I asked, "Who are you and what do you do in here?" The ladies laughed as they realized that I didn't mean to pose my question so awkwardly, but I was truly in a state of shock. In that moment, I felt like it was my sign of confirmation that I should pursue other employment as I had burn out on 3 part-time jobs and a busy school schedule. I smiled and said, "Excuse me. What is career services?"

The lady who greeted me said, "Cher (pronounced Sha' with a short Louisiana "a" sound), in here, we help with job searches and put together our job fairs." Simultaneously, she handed me a list of about 4-5 jobs. I accepted that list and her response then as I didn't know any better, but years of professional experience have taught me that she was one of those people who was in a job role, not a career role. If career services were her career choice, her response would have been more enthusiastic and she would have taken additional time to give me a tour of the office, further explain the services in which I was eligible to participate.

She didn't ask about neither my classification, graduation date, nor my major(s). It was as if they settled into a role where they only "put together our job fairs" twice a year and assisted graduates with job searches by handing them a list of job openings that area employers had ask them to advertise to the students and graduates. That lady, although a nice person, was not interested one bit about providing me any real career services. She was not invested.

That said, career schools will almost stalk you to use their service, although they really hope that you find your own job and just call them to let them know that you are working. This lets them count you as a working graduate for their credentialing purposes. Whether you are a college student/graduate or a career school graduate, USE YOUR CAREER SERVICES. I say, make them earn their paycheck while they invest in you.

Chapter Four

Finally Getting "THAT CALL"-the interview

Ch4: Finally Getting THAT CALL -the interview

Your communication skills are essential for advancing in your quest. Any phone call can make or break your chances of ever seeing the inside of an employer's office if you don't present yourself appropriately in ways beyond the resume. This chapter will assist you in avoiding any telephone faux pas.

Phone etiquette

Keep it simple. A simple hello goes a long way. One would expect that you are professional enough to answer your phone in an eloquent manner. There should not be any "What up", "Yo", "Speak", or any of the other alleged cool terms that some prefer to use.

A great and simple way to answer your phone is *"Hello, this is _____ (insert your name)."*

DO NOT USE THIS CALL TO ASK QUESTIONS ABOUT THE JOB. Save it for the interview. Time is limited, so when an employer calls to set up an interview, be courteous of their time. It is rather rude when you try to gather information or practically have the interview that very moment by phone.

This scenario reminds me of one of the most annoying days ever. During summer 2016, I was interviewing candidates for a position with my employer. I had taken the previous three days to fill my interview schedule. I was motivated to get the position filled by week's end.

I had one candidate, whom I will call Darius. After multiple attempts to reach him, we were finally able to coordinate an appointment. Darius was scheduled to meet with me on a Wednesday afternoon at 1:00pm. I should have known from the hassle to initially contact him that the interview process would also be a hassle.

At approximately 10 minutes before 1pm, Darius called me to tell me that he was lost. That was fine as our location was a little hard to find and the cellular navigational systems were often misdirecting people to turn on the wrong street. As I was giving Darius correct instructions to our office, he suddenly asked, "Miss Katrina, is the position full-time or part-time?" I informed him that it was indeed a full-time overnight position. He then asked, "Is there benefits and how often would I get paid?"

By this time, I grew aggravated and said, "Darius, it appears that you are not interested in meeting with me since you are asking interview questions while you are trying to find the office. We can cancel, now." He stopped me to say that he really needed the job and was just curious.

Because I was still frustrated, I told him that if he was less than 5 minutes away and if he had not arrived within the next 10 minutes, he would be cancelled. He made it within the allotted time frame. I watched him walk from his car to my office. He was wearing baggy and sagging jeans, a wrinkled, faded black t-shirt with high top tennis shoes. His hair looked like it was in the beginning stages of dreads, but his looked very unkempt.

In short, he was unprofessional via presence and phone. Within the first 5 minutes of the interview, I simply couldn't do it. I took off my human resources hat and put on my momma hat. I felt compelled to educate this young man. I was honest with him. I said, "Darius, I can't in good conscience consider you for this position and I want to tell you why because someone has to care enough about you to tell you what you obviously don't know."

Ironically, he was appreciative of my honesty and was openly receptive to my corrective criticism. I pointed out all the things that he had done wrong from the beginning to that moment in my office. I went so far as to express that he arrived for an interview looking like he just rolled out of bed and came straight to meet me. He said that he had because he had not been getting sleep with a new baby in the house.   There is more to this story, but irrelevant to my point.

While Darius' resume presented enough minimum skills I was seeking to get him an invitation to interview, he blew it every step of the way after that. The moral to Darius' story as it relates to this section of the book is simple, just as he should have kept it. He allowed not only his poor phone etiquette to frustrate his interviewer before ever having met, but he followed up with absolutely no interview couth

Below is a list of appropriate questions you may ask during this time (if the information was not provided beforehand):

-Where are you located?   Be sure to repeat the address back to the scheduler.

-Is there a sign outside of the building? If you are like me and need visual directions, ask for landmarks and intersections if needed.

-Is there covered or paid parking required? Many employers that are in towers or downtown areas will have a parking garage of some sort that may require a toll or parking fee.

-Should I bring anything other than my resume? Depending on the nature of the position, you should know if it is valuable or not to bring anything extra. For example, an aspiring fashion designer should be accompanied by their portfolio to showcase their fashion designs.

-Will this be an individual or panel interview? For your preparation, you want to know if the interviewer will be joined by another person. I always encourage applicants to bring at least 3 or 4 copies of their resume with them for instances where a second or third person decides to participate in the meeting.

On the employer side, this saves them (and you) interviewing time. It avoids you having to schedule multiple interviews with 2 other management people later. While this interview type can be a little stressful, it is convenient and expedites the hiring process.

Voicemail Etiquette

Make sure your voicemail is setup and working properly. There is nothing worse than finding out that an employer was trying to contact you, but was unable to leave a message. Something this simple can cause you to lose that employment opportunity. Employers are not going to chase you. Keep in mind that your resume has been selected from a mass of others and if you fail to be available, one of the other applicants will fill your spot on the interview schedule.

Some other pertinent details to file in your mental rolodex regarding your voicemail and phone etiquette.

-No booty bouncing music.
Ringtones and sounds are fun features for you to enjoy on your phone. Do they really benefit you when you are expecting to receive a flux of professional phone calls? NO, NO, and NO!

When an employer calls and is required to leave a message, he/she does not want to be forced to listen to a whole or even a part of a song before being able to state their business. During my career, I have hung up on many voicemails and so will many other employers.

In addition to the song, the last thing you want the caller to hear is the possibility of explicit or vulgar lyrics. If this applies to you, clean it up immediately. Play it safe and remove any outgoing musical entertainment from your phone, at least until after you have secured employment.

-Have a simple & professional outgoing message.

All cell phones are preset with a generic message. If you are unsure of how to present yourself in your outgoing voicemail, resort to the manufacturer default message.

If you like the sound of your own voice, please establish a clear, audible message.

For example: "Hello, this is _____ (your name). I'm unavailable at this time. Please leave a message and a return phone number at the beep."

If you hate your recorded voice, ask a friend to speak the outgoing message for you. That's what friends are for.

-Check your voicemail regularly & return THAT CALL as soon as possible. Close the call by thanking the interviewer or scheduler for contacting you for the opportunity.

Chapter Five:

The
Face-to-Face Meeting

Ch5: The Face-to-Face Meeting

Much like everything else leading to this point, there are steps to making the most of the time and opportunity.

A. The Preparation

1. Drive the route in advance if possible. Have a backup route in case of traffic or construction detours.

2. Select your ensemble the night before to include trying it on. You don't need this step to cause you any undue stress on the day of the interview. If your meeting is scheduled days 2-3 days out, you may want to dry clean your outfit for a crisp and clean appearance. Remember that we tend feel more confident when we look our best.

Because females have such a diverse wardrobe, there are times when it can be a hazy gray line between business attire and party attire. If you must wonder if the clothes are appropriate, they probably are not.

To the ladies, I offer this simple advice. Your outfit should fit tight enough to show you are a woman, but loose enough to show you are a lady. Let me say that again. Your outfit should be tight enough to show you are a woman, but loose enough to show you are a lady.

3. Review your resume. You want to be sure that the person that walks through the interviewer's door is the same person they see on paper, so take time to familiarize yourself with your resume. It seems silly to say, but I must. This is even more important if you did not create your own resume. There is no rule that says an applicant is required to construct his/her own curriculum vitae. Otherwise, professional resume writers wouldn't exist. Taking time to review it also reduces nerves during the meeting.

Although it is your life and your experience, one would think that it would be easy to talk about oneself without issue. That doesn't always happen. For some reason, you may go brain dead when put on the spot by an interview question or what I like to refer to as having a brain fart.

Bud's story was a perfect example of the things you should and should not present in your resume. Let me share another experience I had while interviewing a young man whom I will call Brad. Brad was interested in working on my career services team.   This energetic, twenty-something year old man arrived in a nice tan suit with a crisp white shirt and multi-colored tie. He held a folder and a cell phone in his hand as he sat across from me to start our meeting.

I went through all the interview preliminaries with small talk, etc. I then began asking about experiences listed on his resume. There were one or two places of employment that stood out among the rest based on his length of time in the position, so I wanted to get some clarity.

Although impressed with Brad on paper, there was something about him in person that I couldn't put my finger on. I just knew that he simply was not the best fit for the role. He confirmed my thought when I asked him about his employment at LMN company (not real workplace). He immediately looked shocked and taken aback by my inquiry. He paused for a moment and then slightly stood up to lean across the table to look at my copy of his resume. He asked, "Huh, that's on there?" A part of me wanted to laugh because I wasn't expecting that response, but I also felt sorry for him.

After he clearly was unprepared, I said to him, "Yes Brad. It's on here. Did you forget?" He started laughing as if I had told the best joke ever and said, "Oh, my girlfriend did my resume and I didn't know she put that on there."

I was done after that. There was nothing else he could tell me to even remotely say to sway my opinion of him. I stood up with an outreached hand to shake his and ended the interview. "Thank you for coming in, Brad, "I said, "I appreciate your time, but I advise you to be familiar with your resume the next time you have an interview."

Sadly, he attempted to try to explain why his girlfriend did his resume, but that was not my concern. Again, there is no rule that says that you cannot employ someone else to compose your resume. I was disappointed in his mere lack of preparation; especially after allowing someone else to have such control over how he was professionally presented. It was his responsibility to proofread the document before submitting it to employers.

4. Professional & Personal References

Another part of being prepared for an interview is to have professional references readily available upon request. This somehow confuses people because we all have different opinions of what constitutes professional. In terms of references, one might think it's easy to list a few family members and call it a day.

Many believe that they only need to list those who will just say nice things about them and who better to offer as a reference other than family. This is NOT TRUE to some extent.

The only time it is okay to use a family member(s) for a reference is when you have worked for an extended period time in a family-owned business. It is in these cases where you might have no other choice but to list mom and dad as your supervisors. If the business is or was a little larger and had staff other than family members, I suggest using one of the staff members as a professional reference not a personal one. Using a family member, whether they are valid or not, doesn't provide the clout that a non-family member can bring to the table.

A professional reference is someone who can honestly speak to not only your personality traits, but also to your work ethic, education and training, and their opinion of your eligibility or qualifications for the role you are pursuing. Professional references should be from your pool of current or former co-workers and supervisors. If you have never held a job, it is acceptable to refer to former teachers, college professors or instructors, and even a classmate with whom you have developed a strong professional relationship.

In regards to the classmate option, this person should be someone who preferably had more than one class with you. They should have worked in some form of a group project or collaboration with you. Otherwise, they really offer no valid source of reference.

The key to providing references is to first get their permission. It is professionally proper to ask your selected references for their authorization to be either a professional or personal reference for you. By not doing so, you could be setting yourself up for an embarrassing situation. There is nothing like learning that someone really doesn't like you by way of a reference call. People who don't like or respect you won't give permission to be your reference, so it is to your benefit to ask beforehand. Not to mention, if they agree to be a reference, this provides them with advanced notification that they may be receiving a phone call or an email about you. You can also use this time to verify the spelling of their name, contact information, job title, etc.

This brings me to another anecdote about one of my real-life experiences during my career as a Human Resources Director. For the sake of the story and protecting identities, I will refer to this young lady as Nakee.

She was such a wonderful person. Her heart was genuinely kind. I got to know her well during the time we worked together. Every morning, she would stop by my office to say hello and to ask if I needed anything. During that time, I was pregnant with my first baby and she was quite fond of that and whole-heartedly cared about my well-being. She was a mother of 2 young kids, one was nearing a year old when I met her, so I think she still had "baby fever".

Although Nakee was a joy to be around, she had one flaw. She was hardly ever around. Because she would faithfully pop into my office every morning to ask if I needed anything, it was obvious when she was absent. Nakee had a large attendance issue.

After repeatedly calling in sick, her manager and I were discussing options of handling the matter. She was well-liked, so termination was not an initial thought. It was decided that I would call her references to see if this was a previous problem for her.

Upon hire, she provided three references. I called the first two and had to leave a message to return my call. Finally, I called the last person on her list. A man with a strong, deep voice answered, "Hello," he said. I responded, "Hello. This is Katrina Chretien with so and so employer. May I speak to Rodney Rock (not his real name)?" "This him," he said. I proceeded to tell him that he was listed as a professional reference for Nakee."

Before I could ask if he had a moment to speak with me, he quickly started to laugh. Caught completely off guard by his boisterous laughter, I asked, "Mr. Rock, did I say something funny?" Still laughing, he stated, "Lady, I don't know what Nakee told y'all or got y'all thinking, but I ain't never worked with her and she ain't never worked for me. She is my baby momma."

A brief silence came over the conversation. For a person who is never at a loss for words, I was speechless. That was the first time I had encountered such a situation. In addition, I was in disbelief because it was Nakee. Everyone liked Nakee, so for her to provide a false professional reference was shocking. I was embarrassed for her. After regaining my senses, I ended the call by thanking him for the information and his time. As we were about to hang up, he said, "I don't know what kinda game Nakee playing, but I'll tell her you called."

There's no reason to reiterate this, but I will say it again. It is in your best interest to get your references' permission to use them as such. There is nothing like finding out that the person really didn't like or respect you. For inquiring minds who want to know how this situation ended. I'll keep it short. Nakee returned to work 2 days later and upon arrival, walked into my office and sat in my guest chair. Head down, shoulders hunched forward, with a timid facial expression, she sat quietly like a child awaiting punishment or chastisement from a parent. I replayed the scenario of the phone call back to her. She started to cry. She said, 'Miss Katrina. I really need this job, so when the application asked for 3 references, I couldn't think of a third one, so I just put my little girl's daddy." She went onto tell me that he told her that he had spoken to me.

It was during this time with Nakee that she started telling me about how she had been ill and having a hard time shaking whatever was ailing her. I advised her that she had to submit a doctor's release if she were to be out again for 3 or more days. She understood and apologized repeatedly. That didn't stop her from starting a new cycle of absence just two days later. That's when I received a confidential fax from her physician informing me that she would be out of work and under his care for the following week. Sadly, because of the letterhead, I also learned of what was truly ailing her and causing her excessive absence. My heart sunk as she was indeed very ill and I was unable to discuss it with her management team for confidentiality purposes.

In short, most employers request a standard three professional references. In some cases, you may receive a request for four. Regardless of the requests, it is always best to offer all professional references.

My resume offers a professional reference page to include three of my former supervisors and one colleague. As my career grew and transitioned, so did my references. To date, my reference page has remained the same since 2013. Once your career levels, stagnant, or plateau, you may not have a need to refresh your references as often as you would in the earlier or middle stages of your professional growth and development. I personally suggest that you refresh a few of your references every 3-5 years; especially if you offer a personal reference among the list.

B. The Big Day

Whether you are scheduled for a morning or afternoon interview, be proactive in everything you do. I like to say that you should hope for the best and plan for the worst-case scenario. It would be just your luck that everything falls to pieces on one of the biggest days of your career.

Let's try to keep mishaps at bay by committing to the following strategies:

1. Get your head in the game. Attitude is everything.

2. "As a man thinketh in his heart, so is he"
    (from the King James Bible, Proverbs 23:7).

When I need a little mental pick me up, I refer to two my favorite motivational quotes.

"Finish each day and be done with it. You have done what you could. Some blunders and absurdities no doubt crept in; forget them as soon as you can. Tomorrow is a new day; begin it well and serenely and with too high a spirit to be cumbered with your old nonsense," said literary great, Ralph Waldo Emerson.

*"OBSTACLES don't have to stop you. If you run into a
wall, don't turn around and give up. Figure out how to
climb it, go through it, or work around it," said
professional basketball player, Michael Jordan.*

Beyond reflecting on the quotes, I think about a track and field analogy. Imagine a track meet where the runners are in the starting blocks. At the sound of the gun, they all take off and start building momentum to leap over the hurdles. Whether they are moving at either their fastest or slowest speed, mistakes can happen.

What happens when a hurdler trips? They might fall, even have an injury. They could even fall in someone else's lane; thereby hindering that person's race. No matter what obstacle they face, they get up and finish the race, even if it means they may end in last place. They bounce back and later reflect on areas on improvement for the next time.

While you are getting dressed, listen to the radio, watch the news, or use a traffic app on your cellular phone. You need to be aware of any hold ups on the highway that may interfere with your commute. Not only does having a traffic update aid in the smoothness of your day, but heading to your appointment about 15-20 minutes early also leaves room for any errors that may arise.

Cleanliness is next to Godliness

Looking good doesn't mean you smell good, so please regard the principles of hygiene. Take a shower. Brush your teeth. Do not drench yourself with a half bottle of neither perfumes, colognes, nor scented lotions. That would be more offensive than if you had not bathed or showered. A small dab or squirt of your favorite scent will suffice. It is important not to set off any allergies during your meeting.

 Lastly, **DO NOT SMOKE** after you shower and before the interview. Many smokers tell me that they need that last cigarette to calm their nerves before the appointment. My response to that is always the same, "if you don't get that job, you won't be able to afford anymore cigarettes, so you need to decide which is more important in that moment." In addition, many employers are establishing smoke-free environments, so if you go into said building smelling like an ashtray, you may be considered "not best fit" just because you possess a habit that is not conducive to the company culture.

To Be Early Is To Be On Time;
To Be On Time Is To Be Late

I apply this rule to my daily life not just for scheduled interviews and meetings. I'm passing this on to you; especially if you run on a clock other than the right one. With the possibility of your nerves racing, you need to arrive early to your appointment just so you can have extra time to calm yourself down before entering the building.

I suggest you get there about 10-15 minutes early. If you happen to arrive sooner than that, wait in the car for a little while and review your resume, check your face (teeth and nose), DO NOT SMOKE, and say a little prayer for success.

If you don't know how or what to say, you can borrow mine.

"Lord God, I ask that you grant me a successful interview/meeting. Guide my words, my deeds, and my actions during this appointment and allow that all of it is a testament to how great you are. In the name of Jesus. Amen."

It is important that you know your interview started the moment you parked your car. How is that, you ask? Well, an extremely thorough employer may be waiting and watching for your arrival from their office window. If not, they could have someone else keeping an investigative eye out for the person who seems to be coming in for a scheduled appointment. Even if you aren't being watched, pretend that you are because it will keep you on your toes.

Once you enter the building for your meeting or check in at the front desk, you may be asked to wait. That wait could range anywhere from a few minutes to an hour, depending upon what is happening behind the scenes. Nonetheless, use your wait time wisely. Most people fall prey to pulling out their cellular phones to either call someone, text, play games, or read a magazine while waiting. These are all bad ideas. In fact, you should leave your phone in the car to avoid the temptation. Again, you need to pretend you are being watched, so be productive. To do so, review your resume and your pre-prepared end-of-the-interview questions.

Also, observe your surroundings. Pay attention to the environment. Do the employees seem to be happy there? Is it a comfortable workplace? These observations can also create additional questions to ask during the interview.

The Wait Is Over!

For conversational purposes, let's just say your wait was all of 10-15 minutes. That great; yet nerve-wrecking moment has finally arrived. Upon greeting your interviewer(s), offer a firm, but avoid a hand-breaking, handshake. I suggest that you restate your name just because interviewers, managers, etc. typically have a lot on their minds and you want to ensure they flush their brains of the names of anyone before meeting with you. In addition, give them a fresh copy of your professional resume.

During this time and if you have a little walk ahead of you, the small talk will start. I'm a person who doesn't mind empty silence, but several would drive themselves bonkers if every waking moment isn't filled with chatter. If you are this type, simply comment on the office décor, how easy it was to find the office with your driving directions and conditions, or the safest & traditional topic of the weather. This temporary chit chat should be a warm up to getting to the knitty gritty of the real conversation ahead.

CHAPTER SIX:

The Interview

THE INTERVIEW

There are 3 parts to an interview:

-The Introduction   -The Body   -The Closing

The introduction can be best described as the small talk, but it is much more than that. This part of the session is where the interviewer/employer takes time to tell you a little about who they are, what they do, and for what they are hiring. This is the perfect point where you can show interest in the company by stating something you researched about them on the internet.

The Body is the core of the entire meeting, but it is also the segment that may begin as if it should be in the introduction. Tell me about yourself is a popular starting point with many interviewers. It is also the question that causes candidates to stumble and lose focus.

Let's take a step back for just a minute. People trip up during interviews because they don't know how to respond to a question. So, to avoid that from happening to you, I'm going to give you the most important guidance and tools you will find in this entire book.

I'm going to hand you the instruments needed to convert you into an interview artist.

Tool #1

It doesn't matter how many questions an interviewer ask. The truth is that they are asking you the same question in different versions. The almighty and most important question at the nucleus of every question is the same root question....

WHAT CAN YOU DO THAT WILL MAKE MY BUSINESS MONEY?
-or-
WHAT CAN YOU DO THAT IS A BILLABLE SERVICE FOR MY BUSINESS?

Now, let's think about this for a moment. If you allow this question to navigate your thought process with each interview inquiry, you will find that it will naturally open your mind to appropriate responses.

Let's go back to that good ole' popular starter question:

Tell Me A Little Bit About Yourself.

Traditionally most people respond like this, "Well, my name is _____. I'm ____ years old. I'm single with 3 kids. I love bike riding and I enjoy working with people." After a long pause and rolling their eyes around in a show of defeat, they continue with, "I don't know what else you want to know. I'm hard worker and a good communicator."

How many times have you used a similar response? Effective immediately, you will no longer answer in that manner. Cut it out of your brain. So, how are you supposed to answer this question?

Pay attention because this brings me to my next tool.

Tool#2

Since you understand the root interview question, I now want to layout the correct way of answering said inquiries. Always keep the root questions in your mental rolodex as a guide.

WHAT CAN YOU DO THAT WILL MAKE MY BUSINESS MONEY?
OR
WHAT CAN YOU DO THAT IS A BILLABLE SERVICE FOR MY BUSINESS?

You have two types of answers-concrete and abstract. Most people provide abstract answers to their interview questions. Your response should be primarily made up of concrete answers.

What is the difference between a concrete and an abstract answer?

Here is my logical breakdown. What comes to mind when you think of something concrete? You are correct if words like, hard, firm, and solid popped into your head. What about when you think of something abstract?

If terms like, not firm, needs to be deciphered, or read between the lines, you are right once again. Let me give you my synopsis on the difference as it relates to your interviewing and self-marketing skills.

Your concrete skills are your money-making skills. They are the solid foundation of your billable services and assets. Your concrete skills are your education, your degrees, certifications, licenses, and relevant work experience.

Your abstract skills are the things that most of the public want to sell as solid skills, but they are not. I refer to these skills as fluff. Your abstract skills are your professional characteristics like your attention to detail, ability to be a team player, your time-management capabilities, etc. The fluff alone is no good, but presented with the concrete, you are then presenting yourself as a great employee.

Concrete skills can be presented alone without any abstracts, but abstracts cannot be presented without concrete as they are not a strong and solid foundation to withstand the storm of an interview. They must have support.

If you can't remember how this works, here it is. Seventy-five percent (75%) or more of your interview response should include money-making skills and assets, while the other 25% or less should be the fluff.

Imagine that your interview is a dinner party and you are the host. If you were to serve your guest, the interviewer, a plate of food, that plate should consist of both an entrée' and a few sides. The entrée, the meat, is your main course. This is your concrete dish. Your sides are your vegetables, usually from an a' la' carte menu. They make up the abstract part of the meal. The sides make the entrée' taste so much better, more savory and delicious. No one wants to eat just a plain entrée'.

That said, your interview plate should be filled with both meat and potatoes, per se. One can enjoy a steak all by itself, but in conjunction with a side of vegetable medley and potatoes, the mouth just starts to water. That is what you want to offer at your interview-a healthy portion of what you bring to the table.

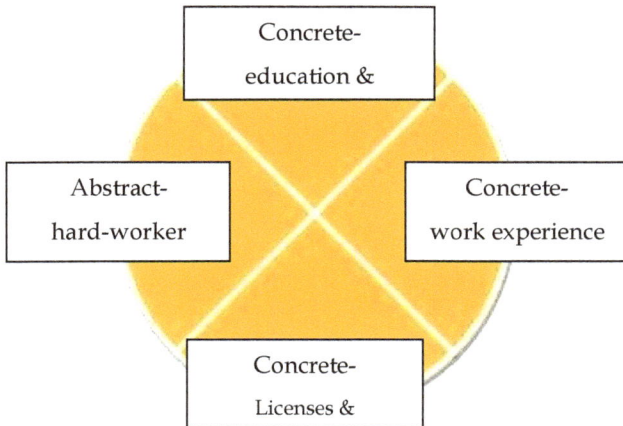

Once you grasp an idea of what you will serve at your dinner party, it becomes a breeze to host event after event.

Let's practice preparing your plate.

<u>Practice Exercise</u>

Below you will see a list of some basic and most commonly asked interview questions. Take a moment to answer each question as you would in a real interview. As you go through the exercise, try implementing your recently learned skills with concrete and abstract skills.

Tell me a little bit about yourself.

_____
_____
_____
_____

Why should I hire you?

_____

_____

_____

_____

_____

What do you consider to be your professional strength?

_____

_____

_____

_____

What do you consider to be your professional weakness?

_____

_____

_____

_____

If I were to speak with your supervisor, what would they tell me about you?

_____

_____

_____

_____

_____

Take a moment to review your responses again. Did you provide 75% or more of concrete assets and 25% or less of your abstract skills? If not, what else could you have included in or deleted out of your self-marketing pitch?

Review some example responses, which may aid you in molding your frame of thinking as you officially adopt your own natural interview responses to these questions.

The examples below do not consist of any real information associated with any known person(s) or places. That said, you can use these sample responses and adjust them to fit who you are.

Tell me a little bit about yourself.

 As my resume indicates, I am a graduate from RST University with a bachelor's degree in a mass communications with a minor in english. Over the past 6 years, I have acquired news and feature writing experience as a staff writer with the Candyland Express newspaper in the town of Friendship, USA. From beat assignment to printing, I handle all aspects of my articles. I also do my own photography for my stories. At this time, I am seeking an opportunity of growth that is not currently available with my current employer as we are a small publication with an equally small circulation.

Why should I hire you?

 I am the best person for you to hire because not only have I completed the formal education of an industrial engineer, I have also invested additional time and expense in getting certified in the following engineering programs-Six Sigma, AutoCad, Linux, and Open R, to name a few. My 4 years of experience with P-A-L Engineering Firm has granted me multiple opportunities to design and quality test industrial tools and equipment for 3 of our major offshore rig accounts owned by Boom Shores, Penny Quarters, and Pork Jay. In short, my passion for my field makes me a sponge for continued growth and development while still using my efficient organizational and time management skills for timely project completion.

What do you consider to be your professional strength?

 I believe my professional strength to date is my years of experience as a retail manager. For the past 16 years, I have not only managed multiple high end boutiques and staffs ranging from 8-35 employees, but I have also work closely with the owners to develop an efficient method of marketing and branding those stores. I train my staff to provide quality customer service, while I study shopping trends, and metrics to boost revenue and profits.

What do you consider to be your professional weakness?

Because I am such a team player, I have found that my weakness is just that. I tend to want to fix everything for everyone and I end up taking on more tasks than I am able to handle in a timely manner. I have a hard time saying, "no", but I have vowed that this year will be different and I am slowly starting to set boundaries and limitations on my available time.

If I were to speak with your supervisor, what would they tell me about you?

Well, I can't really speak for them, but based upon my performance feedback from them, you would be told that I am a skilled middle school teacher because I create diverse lesson plans that satisfy diverse learning styles. My students successfully test and pass state required tests within the above average percentile because I assess all of my students not only based upon behavior, but also their strengths and weaknesses. This helps me to curtail my teaching methods to accommodate each student. I am proactive in developing and nurturing teacher-parent relationships, and have received my school's Teacher-Of-The-Year award for the past 5 years.

We're all different and so are our communication styles. The key to this chapter is to emphasize the proper usage of your concrete and abstract skills. Go back to my sample responses with 2 different color hi-lighters or ink pens.

Use one color to circle the money-making skills in each answer and use the other color to identify the fluff skills. The more you can identify which is which, the faster it will become to fill those silent moments during your interview. You won't need to spend as much time trying to gather your thoughts before providing an answer to your interviewer.

Tool #3

Knowing how to highlight your skills is a paramount tool, but it doesn't negate the fact that you still need to know how to effectively answer the core interview questions. These answers are known as STARS. You now know how to prepare your meal for your metaphorical dinner party. The food is only a small part of the function. You still need to fine tune the other details that will complete the event package-room set up, table setting, flatware and silverware, background music, etc.

STARS is an acronym associated with a prominent interview technique known as Targeted Selected or Behavioral Interviewing. This style of interviewing is designed to assess your ability to handle various workplace situations. With each question asked by the interviewer, you are graded based upon your response.

That grade reflects the way you answered the questions. Interviewers are listening for STAR responses.

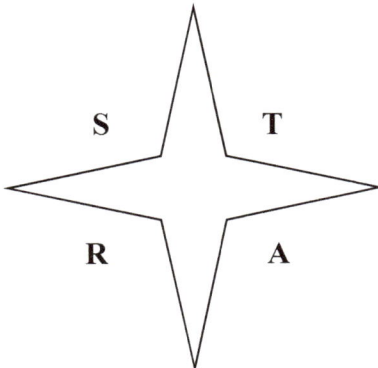

A STAR response is a complete answer to a question involving your actions while dealing with a variety of situations and experiences. They should never be generalized as most people tend to do. As the interviewer, an appropriate and complete answer must consist of the following: **Situation or Task, Action, and Result**. Your responses should be strictly about you and your experience.

The employer does not care about what anyone else did in the given situation, only you. This means that you must think before you speak because it would be easy to talk yourself into a corner if you lose focus of each questions' purpose. So, allow these questions to stream your mind. What did I do in that scenario? What did I contribute to that situation? Be mindful that if you don't possess a specific work example or experience you can also utilize school situations. The key is that you can show leadership and proactivity skills.

Here are some examples questions with STAR responses. See if you can pick out the STAR in each answer.

Question#1

Tell me about a time when you worked as a part of a team and someone on the team was not doing their part.

When I was in college, my journalism instructor assigned a group research project. I was in a team of 5 students and I was team leader. Each person selected which parts they wanted to research and report. Each person also had a deadline to meet, so I could combine all the work and build the display boards to accompany each section of the research. One girl was rarely in class and only showed to 2 out of 6 of our group brainstorm meetings. After she missed 3 meetings and would take days to reply to my emails and texts, I saw her in the parking lot and decided to address my concerns.

She started crying and told me that her life was hectic during that time (no babysitter, car trouble, and recent loss of job). She was falling behind in all her classes and was thinking about dropping out. I felt sorry for her and asked if there was anything I could do to help her meet her deadline with our class. She pulled out a folder of notes and research that she completed weeks before and gave it to me.

She wasn't able to finish combining all of her notes. After she was crying and repeatedly apologizing for inconveniencing the group, I told her that I will take what she completed and put together her final draft since my part could not be done until everyone else submitted their reports to me. She was very grateful. In the end, we received an A on the project.

Did you notice the STAR in the answer above?

-What is the Situation or Task (S or T)? My college journalism class had a team project to complete. One girl was slacking in her team responsibilities by missing class, team meetings, and displaying poor communication with the team.

-What is the Action (A)? As team leader, I attempted to contact her without luck and used a run-in in the parking lot to talk to her and find out what was happening and to learn of her intentions for the group.

-**What is the Result (R)?** I found out she wasn't simply blowing us off, but was really having a tough time in her personal life. I offered to help her with our project by taking on her incomplete assignment in addition to my own. The team didn't have to suffer and we all received an A.

Question#2

Give me an example of a time when you failed to meet a deadline.

When I was an office manager at a dental office, my monthly metrics report was due by 4pm on a Friday. This particular day was hectic as all of our appointments were running late, which meant I couldn't submit my final office revenue report until all patients had been treated and paid for services rendered.

At 3pm, I noticed that I was not going to meet the deadline, so I phoned my manager to let her know about my unforeseen delay. She was understanding and told me to submit it before 6pm as her portion was due by 7pm. Our last patient was completed at about 5:30pm and I was able to submit my report before 6pm.

Did you notice the STAR in the answer above?

-What is the Situation or Task (S or T)? As an office manager, my monthly report was due by 4pm on a Friday. Due to late patient appointments and information needed from those treatments, my report could not be completed by the deadline.

-What is the Action (A)? Upon realizing that I would not be able to meet the deadline, I called my manager to let her know and the reason for the delay.

-What is the Result (R)? My manager understood and extended my deadline by 2 hours. I completed my report with an hour to spare.

The STAR method seems a little perplex at first until you make it one of your regular, best interview practices. So, let's go on a star search. I will list a few popular behavioral questions and you should provide your best STAR responses. Once you have stated your response, follow up by identifying each part of the STAR.

Practice Exercise:

Question#1

Give me an example of a time when you made a decision that didn't offer favorable results.

_____
_____
_____
_____

-What is the Situation or Task?

_____

_____

_____

_____

-What is the Action?

_____

_____

_____

_____

-What is the Result?

_____

_____

_____

_____

Tell me about a time you when you had to go beyond the call of duty to get a job done?

_____

_____

_____

_____

_____

_____

_____

-What is the Situation or Task?

_____
_____
_____
_____

-What is the Action?

_____
_____
_____
_____

-What is the Result?

_____
_____
_____
_____

Give me an example of a time when you had to bend or break the rules to accomplish your goal?

_____
_____
_____
_____
_____
_____

-What is the Situation or Task?

_____

_____

_____

_____

-What is the Action?

_____

_____

_____

_____

-What is the Result?

_____

_____

_____

_____

The question and answer part of your interview is the core. Once you get through the core, the rest should be a breeze with a few other useful tips. Just stay focused and never let them see you sweat. Interviewers will sometimes put you in the "hot seat" just to see how well you handle pressure or uncomfortable situations.

Tool #4

As your interview starts to wind down, a second Q&A segment begins. This time, the interviewer puts you in the driver's seat. It is your moment to show your true interest in both the organization and the position for which you are interviewing.

Following the hiring manager's final core question, you should expect the closing question. Do you have any questions? So often, candidates are so nervous and happy to get the meeting over and done with, that they simply say, "No, I don't." NO! NO! NO! You should never leave an interview without having asked any questions.

Before going to your interview, I suggested that you do your homework by researching the company. From there, you should be able to construct at least three questions of interest for the interviewer. Along with copies of your resume, it is acceptable to take a list of prewritten questions with you to the interview. This is where you can show the employer that the opportunity is significant to your professional goals. It also shows preparedness.

If you don't get a chance to view the company website prior to your meeting, I am more than willing to loan you a few of my safe questions. You will be ready the next time an interviewer ask, "do you have any questions?" You will never have to say. "No, I don't" ever again. Instead, that reply will be more like, "Sure. You answered some of them during the interview, but I have just a few more." Then you can start your query. Don't feel obligated to ask all your questions in the first interview. Ask about 3-4 (maybe 5) of them and save the rest for a potential second round of interviews.

Here are my safe end-of-the-interview questions (if they aren't addressed previously):

Question #1: What is the hiring process for this position?

Question#2: What is the ladder of growth from this role?

Question#3: Why is this position available? Is it a replacement or a new position?

Question#4: How often will my performance be reviewed?

Question#5: What is the company's plan for the next 3-5 years?

Question#6: How long have you worked for this company?

Question7: What do you like about working here?

Question8: Describe the company culture.

Question#9: Describe a typical day for the person in this
position.

Question#10: What do you think is the most challenging
part of this positon and why?

 Can you think of any other questions you can ask? List them
below.

1._____

_____

2._____

_____

3._____

_____

4._____

_____

5._____

_____

After officially ending the meeting, shake the interviewer's
hand and express your gratitude for being considered and the
opportunity to interview. Just because you are about to leave the
meeting, does not mean that the interview is over. Don't forget that
you are still being observed until you leave the property.

That said, review my **Do Not** list:

-**Do Not** pull out your cell phone while in the building.

-**Do Not** stand outside the building to smoke. Wait until
 you exit the parking lot.

-If you were referred by a friend, **Do Not** try to visit them
 in the office. Just leave.

Although there are quite a few do nots, here a few things to
remember to do after leaving.

Don't forget to:

-Send a thank you email or card to the interviewer(s)
 within 48 hours of the meeting.

-If you were referred, be sure to extend a thank you email or card to
that person.

-Don't put all your eggs in one basket. Keep marketing yourself to
other employers until you have officially accepted a position.

CHAPTER SEVEN

I Got the Job,
Now What?

CH7: I Got the Job, Now What?

Congratulations! Receiving the job offer is both the goal and reward for all your hard work. Take some time to relish the moment, exhale, and try to have a night out to celebrate. Once the celebration is over, your next level of work starts.

If you are a recent graduate embarking on a new career journey, you may be faced with a list of things to sort out as you officially launch your new career. It's time to start the balancing act of decisions and choices upon decisions and choices. What are your priorities? If you don't have a clue, take a moment to draft a quick list. Rank them in order of importance. If you need a little help getting started, use my list below and prioritize them from 1-6.

_____Home	_____Work	_____School
_____Family	_____Friends	_____ME

Other decisions you will encounter are paramount in that they are money and time management. Based upon the list above and their level of importance to you, ask yourself one question. How will I split my time between these obligations? Only you can choose how you maintain your balance of these priorities, so don't let this overwhelm you.

A new career and a paycheck (sometimes bigger) spells independence for most, which is why money management is essential to establish in the beginning. It is so easy to fall prey to having Cadillac taste with a Volkswagen budget. I won't spend much time on this topic, but I want to share a friend's story of just how simple it can be to lose yourself with money. While not his real name, I will call him Dre for the sake of making a point.

Dre was a great, intelligent guy from an average, working, middle class family. Both his parents were high school teachers. Because Dre was so smart, he went to college on both an academic and an athletic scholarship. He wanted to venture away from a career in education. Instead he chose to study Mechanical Engineering. In just short of 5 years, Dre graduated from college. He had plans to relocate to a new city, where he felt he would have more career success. It also didn't hurt that he knew a few friends from the area, to include his girlfriend of two years.

It didn't take long for Dre to secure a mechanical engineering position with an offshore equipment supplier. While his position was entry level, his paycheck seemed almost unreal for a new graduate. He accepted a comfortable salary of $75,000 per year. Many of his fellow engineering graduates were barely getting offers beyond the $45k-$50k range. Unlike several of his friends, he completed school without collecting student loan debt, so that made his new income seem even larger. After bunking with a friend for his first month of employment, Dre got his own apartment. He rented a luxury condo with all the bells and whistles.

He allowed his girlfriend to max out his only credit card to decorate it for him. She used every dime of the $5000 limit. Dre was excited! He loved his new job, the money seemed endless, and it always seemed that by the time he spent one paycheck, it was time to receive another. Life was good. In fact, it was so good, he even got new car. After driving around in his dad's 12-year-old, hand-me-down truck, he upgraded himself to a brand-new sports utility vehicle. It too, had all the bells and whistles.

Within 3 months of graduating from college, receiving an extraordinary job offer, relocating to a new city and finding complete independence and freedom from his parents, Dre started to get a little carried away with his spending. He became known as the "big baller" among his friends because he was good to pick up the $250 check at the restaurant for his table of four. He didn't blink twice to pay the bar tab at a nightclub. His girlfriend was always gifted something beautiful and expensive. For their 3-year anniversary, he gave her an engagement ring, but it was hidden inside a new Gucci handbag. He seemed to have it all together in both his personal and professional life.

After 6 months of employment, Dre's benefits became effective with his employer. Upon his parents' advisement, he contributed 15% of his paycheck to a 401k plan. He also had a full benefits package deduction for insurance. Dre never considered that the amount of his paycheck would decrease after his benefits started. That amount was equitable to what he used to "play with" or "toss around".

Not only did he have luxury rent with a monthly club membership, a car note and its' costs, a credit card bill, his daily living expenses, but also he was lovingly paying his girlfriend's student loan payments while she sought better paying employment.

Once he put all the figures on paper and paid attention to his debt to income ratio, reality slapped him hard in the face. He was forced to not only prioritize his personal life, but to develop a non-existent money management plan. That meant he needed to start setting boundaries and relinquish the "big baller" title.

For another few months, he struggled with getting his plan off the ground and finally broke down to get help and guidance from his parents. They showed him how to live comfortably within his means. He kept his car. As soon as his first condo lease ended, he moved into a lesser expensive apartment, significantly reduced his party life and big spending, established a quick payoff plan for the credit card, and he had to break the news to his girlfriend (now fiancée) that he could only afford to help with $150 of her monthly student loan debt. As he explained, "it was so he could start saving for their future together" and any untimely emergencies. Dre's parents saved him in a sense.

The good thing is that as soon as he recognized that he was in a big bind, he entrusted his parents to help him figure it out. Let me be clear here. Don't have Cadillac taste with a Volkswagen budget.

Like Dre and so many others, I went through my own financial heartache in the beginning of my career. To be honest, it was not until I was married with children that my husband and I adopted a financial plan based upon the teachings of Financial Expert, Dave Ramsey's Financial Peace University. The program created such an insurmountable freedom in our budget and money management. It reshaped our financial priorities.

There are many other financial management plans to consider. Some of the other and equally popular financial gurus, to name a few are: Suze Orman, Larry Burkett, Clark Howard, and Robert Kiyosaki. Although the Dave Ramsey plan was ideal for me and my family goals, everyone doesn't need or want to invest in such programs. This information is something you can always file in your mental rolodex for future use or to share with a friend

Well, you've done it, my friend. You have sold your abilities to the employer and landed the position. It is now time to "put up or shut up," per se. All eyes will be on you to produce everything that both you and your resume said you could. As a newcomer to any team, there will be some nervousness and self-doubt. Own your skills and talents with confidence.

Please know that it is okay to be a novice long as you haven't portrayed yourself as anything more in the field. It is also fine to admit when you don't know or understand. It is better to ask a question and receive clear guidance than not to ask a question and make a horrible mistake.

Chapter Eight:

I Didn't Get the Job, Now What?

CH8: I Didn't Get the Job, Now What?

There's not much to say here. Life goes on. Rinse and Repeat the process until you get what you want.

###

About the Author Through the Eyes of Others

"Katrina's passion for workforce quality is apparent in her focus to know and act on those factors that create and maintain satisfaction in the workplace. She has aptly demonstrated this passion by her initiative to convert her Human Resource Career Development lecture series into a Career Development book suitable to help individuals "boot" or "reboot" their career. I have no doubt that this initiative will materially improve employee preparedness.

Katrina is a super example of one who passionately works for an efficient organization. Her focus in tirelessly managing the very best interests of both the employee and management in achieving organizational goals that serves the entire organization! Everyone is definitely well-served to have her with her passion, focus, and professional qualifications as their manager, leader, coach. Good Luck Katrina! You deserve the best!!"

> Martin "Bill" McIntire,
> Former Branch Manager,
> Team Exceed, Dallas, TX

"When Ripple Recovery Ranch decided to integrate Katrina's Career Development Class into our adult Substance Abuse/Co-Occurring Rehab program schedule, a whole new dimension of hope emerged for our clients.

As the Admissions Director, I have had multiple clients come up to me unsolicited to report that they were going to be able to leave our Rehab with a resume and/or job leads in hand; others report feeling empowered to face career transition issues now rather than feeling overwhelmed at the thought of returning to work after rehab; all because of the knowledge, insight and personal empowerment they felt Katrina provided them with.

Incorporating a Career Development Class, supplemented by her Individual Career Consulting offered to clients, Katrina has become quite popular on our campus. Adding this therapeutic practical service to our clients has no doubt given us an edge in our treatment approach. With Katrina's expertise, we are empowering and equipping adults to have productive, successful lives as they embark on their recovery journey after discharge. I highly recommend this book from a career development expert and coach."

-Donna Tiemeyer, Admissions Director,
Ripple Recovery Ranch, Spring Branch, TX

"As a former instructor at Texas Women's University, I didn't hesitate to invite and welcome Career Development Coach & Expert, Katrina Chretien, to provide some career and life skills lectures to my students. Both her enthusiasm and delivery of pertinent information makes for a
 captivating presentation of real life situations & examples that can last a lifetime! Her calming coaching style and natural sense of humor is something you will never forget!"

-Texas Woman's University, Family Science Instructor,
  Ronniesha R. Bivens, BSHESC'02, MSHESC'04

"I had the privilege of working alongside Katrina years ago at Progressive Insurance. Not only was Katrina reliable, professional, dependable, and knowledgeable, she mastered her crafts well, specializing in Human Resources. Her customer service orientation and easy connection to people took her places, literally, while traveling for the company to seek and hire top talent for the organization, much like herself. She has since transitioned to new endeavors and maintains the same energy, reliability and knowledge that enables her to coach, mentor, and educate others in the field of career development and career launching".

   -Tonja Augmon-Bennett, Former Casualty Claims
    Adjuster, Progressive Insurance, Richardson, TX.

Dear Reader,

Thank you for buying my book. This purchase represents so many different things for you.

Whether it is for yourself or a gift to someone else, you have chosen to invest in something invaluable for the recipient-their professional career development and goals.

I look forward to retaining your readership, so I invite you to periodically visit both my career coaching website at http://careercoachkwc/webstarts.com and also my publisher's website at http://gandmpub.wixsite.com/gloucesterandmidland to keep abreast of upcoming works and events.

                                        Best Regards & Be Blessed,
                                        Katrina Chretien, Author

The
Interview Artist

www.ingramcontent.com/pod-product-compliance
Lightning Source LLC
Chambersburg PA
CBHW042128080426

42735CB00001B/8